Selections from

SHARING *the* SEASON
VOLUME I

Table of Contents

Note: All instrumental accompaniments are strictly optional.

I Saw Three Ships

I saw three ships come sailing in
On Christmas Day, on Christmas Day.
I saw three ships come sailing in
On Christmas Day in the morning.

And what was in those ships all three
On Christmas Day, on Christmas Day?
And what was in those ships all three
On Christmas Day in the morning?

The Virgin Mary and Christ were there
On Christmas Day, on Christmas Day;
The Virgin Mary and Christ were there
On Christmas Day in the morning.

— Traditional

Jesu, Joy of Man's Desiring

Jesu, Joy of man's desiring,
Is my Refuge and my Stay.
Him I love, He is my Lifespring
And my Health and Strength alway.
I have Jesu, who doth love me;
His great love doth help me daily.
Ah, my Jesu is my Friend,
Him I trust, on Him depend.

Jesu now my Joy remaineth,
Bringeth comfort, peace, relief;
Jesu me rich pleasure sendeth,
Him I thank, in Him believe.
Jesu is my All, my sunshine,
He's my Savior and my Lifeline.
I will not from Jesu part,
He will dwell within my heart.

— Chorale text by Martin Jahn
English version by W.E. Buszin

Oh Come Little Children

Oh come, little children, from cot and from hall;
Oh come to the manger in Bethlehem's stall.
There meekly he lieth the heavenly Child,
So poor and so humble, so sweet and so mild.

The hay is His pillow, the manger His bed;
The beasts stand in wonder to gaze on His head.
Yet there where He lieth, so weak and so poor,
Come shepherds and wise men to kneel at His door.

Now "Glory to God" sing the angels on high,
"And peace upon earth" heav'nly voices reply.
Then come, little children, and join in the lay
That gladdened the world on that first Christmas Day.

— Christoph von Schmidt

Oh, Holy Night

Oh, holy night, the stars are brightly shining;
It is the night of the dear Savior's birth.
Long lay the world in sin and error pining,
Till He appeared and the soul felt its worth.
A thrill of hope, the weary soul rejoices,
For yonder breaks a new and glorious morn.
Fall on your knees, Oh, hear the angel voices!
Oh night divine, Oh night when Christ was born!
Oh night, Oh holy night, Oh night divine!

Led by the light of faith serenely beaming,
With glowing hearts by His cradle we stand.
So led by light of a star sweetly gleaming,
Here came the wise men from the Orient land.
The King of Kings lay in lowly manger,
In all our trials born to be our friend.
He knows our need, To our weakness no stranger.
Behold your King! before the lowly bend!
Behold your King! your King! before Him bend!

Truly He taught us to love one another;
His law is love and His gospel is peace.
Chains shall He break, for the slave is our brother,
And in His name all oppression shall cease.
Sweet hymns of joy in grateful chorus rise we,
Let all within us praise His holy name.
Christ is the Lord, Then ever, ever praise we;
His pow'r and glory ever more proclaim,
His pow'r and glory ever more proclaim.

— John Sullivan Dwight

What Child Is This

What child is this, who, laid to rest,
On Mary's lap is sleeping?
Whom angels greet with anthems sweet,
While shepherds watch are keeping?

Refrain
This, this is Christ the King,
Whom shepherds guard and angels sing;
Haste, haste to bring him laud,
The Babe, the son of Mary.

Why lies he in such mean estate
Where ox and ass are feeding?
Good Christian, fear; for sinners here
The silent Word is pleading

So bring him incense, gold, and myrrh,
Come peasant, king, to own him;
The King of kings salvation brings,
Let loving hearts enthrone him.

— William Chatterton Dix

Lorie Line

Selections from

Sharing *the* Season

Volume I

Piano Arrangements by Lorie Line

Edited by Paul Maybery

© 1994 Time Line Productions, Inc.

222 Minnetonka Avenue South, Wayzata, MN 55391
612-474-1000

All Rights Reserved

Dedication...

My fans first discovered me making a living, playing the piano for a department store in Minneapolis. When I'd play, they'd stop to talk. And we became friends. This project is dedicated to all the shoppers who took notice and discovered me.

Notes from the Artist...

There were so many requests to publish my arrangements of music that in 1992, I published the title track to "Threads of Love." It was the first piece to actually get written down for another pianist to play, and the response was overwhelming. Music stores everywhere told me it was even more popular than "Heart and Soul" (the fun piece kids play everywhere when they get together). I continued on and published "Sharing the Season, Volume II," then "Walking With You," and the latest, "The Heritage Collection, Volume I." Everywhere my published arrangements turned up, everyone kept asking,"Where's Sharing the Season, Volume I?" I explained that publishing sheet music started after this project was created, and that maybe some day I'd go back and publish the first album in sheet music form. The requests for the music were so consistent that this year I dedicated the fall season to going back, re-living the recording and writing down the notes I played in the studio in 1991.

The album, Sharing the Season, was the one that launched my career. It's sentimental to me. As I reflected during the creation of this book, I realized there was just something magical about this music. Whatever nostalgia and excitement this project brought to me in the making, I hope you'll also experience in the playing.

May this music inspire you. And may you enjoy it for many holidays to come.

Lorie Line

Christmas, 1994

I Saw Three Ships

Traditional
Arranged by LORIE LINE
Edited by Paul Maybery

Copyright © 1991 Time Line Productions, Inc.
222 Minnetonka Avenue South
Wayzata, Minnesota 55391
All Rights Reserved

First Ending
Fine Ending
Fine
First Ending
Fine Ending
Fine

45
45
51
mp
51
57
mp
57
63
63

69
75
81
D
A7/D
D
A7/D
D
87
A
D
A7/D
D
A7

93
D
A
D
93
99
mf
99
104
D
A7/D
D
A7/D
D
8va
mf
104
110
A
D
A7/D
D
A7
8va
110

116
D
A7/D
D
8va
116
122
8va
Loco
122
128
D
A7/D
D
A7/D
D
128
134
A
D
A7
134

D
A7
D
D(No3)
f
f
(Drone)

163
A(No3)
D
163
169
mf
D
mf
169
175
A7/D
D
A7/D
D
A
175
181
D
A7
D
A7/D
D
181

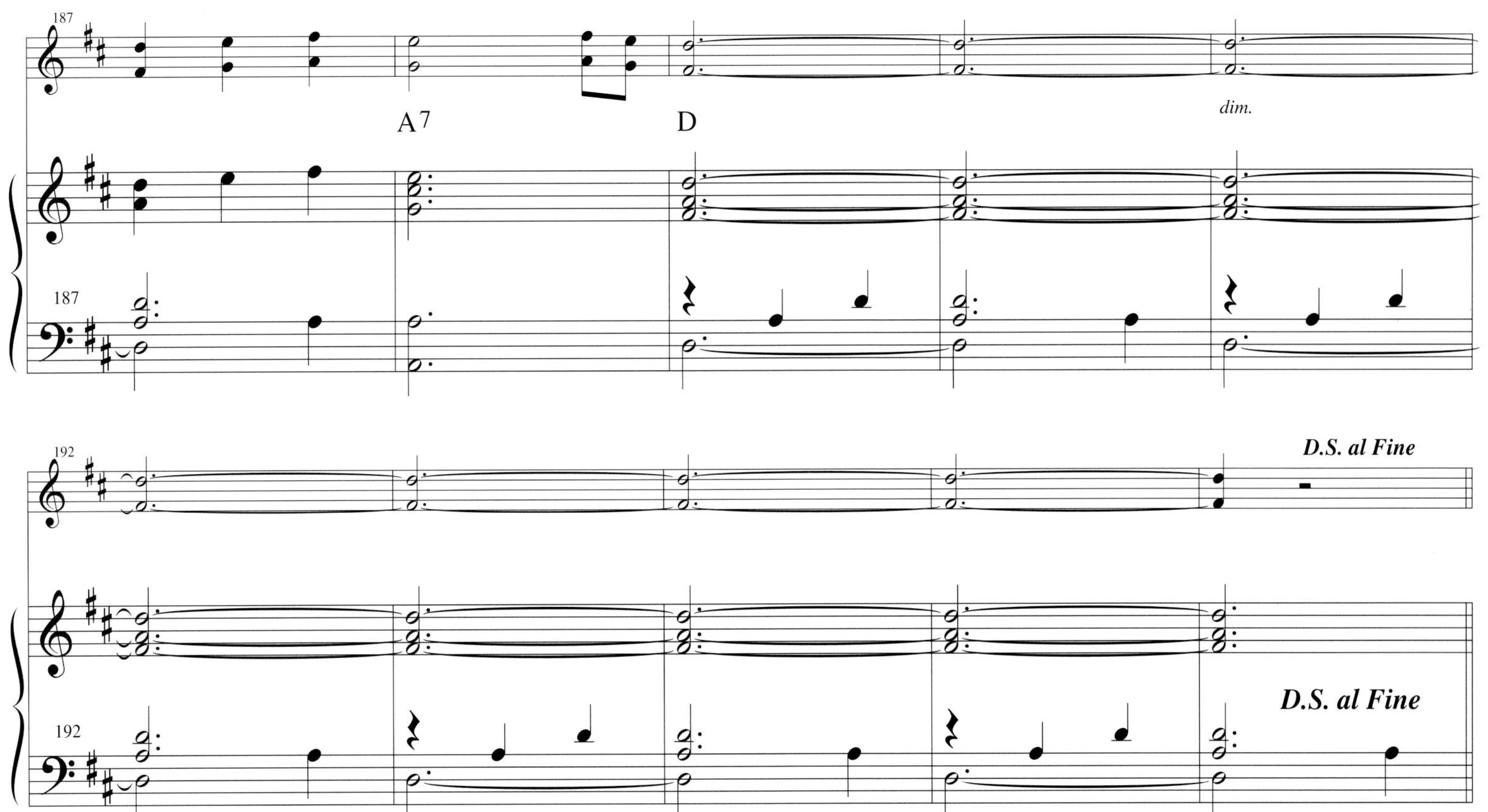
187
A7
D
dim.
187
192
D.S. al Fine
192
D.S. al Fine

Recorders, Flutes, or Violins

I Saw Three Ships

Traditional
Arranged by LORIE LINE
Edited by Paul Maybery

Copyright © 1991 Time Line Productions, Inc.
222 Minnetonka Avenue South
Wayzata, Minnesota 55391
All Rights Reserved

115
123
128
131
139
147
151
f
155
163
171
174
mf
179
187
D.S. al Fine
dim.

Oh Come Little Children

J.A.P. Schulz
Arranged by LORIE LINE
Edited by Paul Maybery

Copyright © 1991 Time Line Productions, Inc.
222 Minnetonka Avenue South
Wayzata, Minnesota 55391
All Rights Reserved

D7 G G D7 G Am7 D7
13
Ped. Ped. Ped. [as needed]
mp
G C G/B Em Am7 G/D D7 G G
17
mp
D7 G G D7 G Am7 D7
21
G/B C G/B Em Am7 G/D D7 G G
25
28

D7 G G D7 G Am7 D7
29
G/B C G/B Em Am7 G/D D7 G A
33
mf
mf
E7 A A E7 A Bm E7
37
A/C♯ D A/C♯ F♯m Bm A/E E7 A
41
rit.
p
rit.
p

Recorders, Flutes, or Violins

Oh Come Little Children

J.A.P. Schulz
Arranged by LORIE LINE
Edited by Paul Maybery

Copyright © 1991 Time Line Productions, Inc.
222 Minnetonka Avenue South
Wayzata, Minnesota 55391
All Rights Reserved

Oh, Holy Night

Adolphe Charles Adam
Arranged by LORIE LINE
Edited by Paul Maybery

Copyright © 1991 Time Line Productions, Inc.
222 Minnetonka Avenue South
Wayzata, Minnesota 55391
All Rights Reserved

E♭
Gm/E♭
E♭6
Cm
Gm
Fm
Cm
E♭/B♭
B♭7
Cm
E♭
E♭/B♭
B♭7
E♭
B♭
E♭
A♭
E♭/B♭
B♭7
E♭/B♭
E♭
E♭
B♭/D
A♭
Cm

Gm/B♭
A♭
Gm
Fm7
B♭7
Gm7
B♭
A♭
Cm
Gm/B♭
Gm
Gm
8va
A♭/B♭
f
E♭
A♭/B♭
B♭7
E♭
Cm
sfz
sfz
sfz
Gm
sfz
sfz
sfz
Fm
sfz
sfz
sfz
Cm
sfz

E♭/B♭
B♭7
Cm
A♭
E♭
A♭/B♭
B♭7
E♭
B♭
Gm7
A♭
ff
sfz
sfz
sfz
sfz
sfz
sfz
sfz
E♭/B♭
B♭
E♭
B♭/D
A♭
E♭
mp
dim. e rit.
pp

Jesu, Joy of Man's Desiring

J.S. Bach
Arranged by LORIE LINE
Edited by Paul Maybery

Copyright © 1991 Time Line Productions, Inc.
222 Minnetonka Avenue South
Wayzata, Minnesota 55391
All Rights Reserved

G Bm/F♯ C/E G/D G/C G/B C A/C♯ G/D D7
G
G Bm/F♯ C/E D/F♯ C/E D
C D7/F♯ G D D7 D
G Bm/F♯ C/E Bm Em7 Am D D7
G Bm/F♯ C/E Em7 G/C G/B C A/C♯ G/D

E♭
F7
B♭
B♭
E♭/G
cresc.
ritard
f
A tempo
F/A
E♭/G
F
E♭/G
F/A
B♭
F
E♭/F
E♭/G
F7
B♭
Dm/A
E♭/G
Dm/A
Dm
Gm7
Cm
F
B♭
E♭/G
mf
B♭/F
B♭/E♭
B♭/D
E♭
E○
B♭/F
B♭
Molto ritardando

What Child Is This

Traditional
Arranged by LORIE LINE
Edited by Paul Maybery

Copyright © 1991 Time Line Productions, Inc.
222 Minnetonka Avenue South
Wayzata, Minnesota 55391
All Rights Reserved

16
16
21
Bm
G
F♯m
Bm
C
21
mf
26
Am
B
B
Bm
G
26
31
F♯m
Bm7
C
B
Esus4
31

Em
mp
mp
[Guitar Lead]
mf
mp
8va

56
56
61
mf
mf
61
66
66
71
71

76
mp
mp
76
81
8va
mf
81
G
86
Em
D
Bm
C
Am
86
91
B
B
G
E
D
91

96
Bm
C
B7
Esus4
Em
96
101
Bm
G
F♯m
Bm
C
f
101
106
A
B
B
Bm
G
106
111
D/F♯
Bm
C
B7
Esus4
111

Em
mp
mp
8va
ritard.
ritard.

Guitar

What Child Is This

Traditional
Arranged by LORIE LINE
Edited by Paul Maybery

Copyright © 1991 Time Line Productions, Inc.
222 Minnetonka Avenue South
Wayzata, Minnesota 55391
All Rights Reserved

55
61
mf
67
73
mp
79
85
G
Em
D
Bm
C
Am
91
B
B
G
E
D
Bm
97
C
B7
Esus4
Em
Bm
G
103
F♯m
Bm
C
A
B
B
109
Bm
G
D/F♯
Bm
C
B7
115
Esus4
Em
mp
121
ritard.

Order Forms

Time Line releases are available at gift shops and music retailers across the country. If you can't find the album you're looking for, ask your local retailer, or use the order form below.

TITLE	Cassettes	QTY	CDs	QTY	TOTAL
The Heritage Collection Volume I	$11.00		$16.00		
Walking With You	$11.00		$16.00		
Beyond a Dream	$11.00		$16.00		
Sharing the Season Volume II	$11.00		$16.00		
Sharing the Season Volume I	$11.00		$16.00		
Threads of Love	$11.00		$16.00		
Storyline	$11.00		$16.00		
Out of Line	$11.00		$16.00		
PUBLISHED SHEET MUSIC OF RECORDINGS					
The Heritage Collection Volume I			$16.00		
"Walking With You" Original Music			$16.00		
Sharing the Season Volume II			$16.00		
Sharing the Season Volume I			$16.00		
"Threads of Love" Title Track			$6.00		
				Sub Total	
				In MN add 6.5% tax	
				Shipping	
				TOTAL	

Shipping in the U.S. is $1.50 for the first item, plus 50 cents for each additional item. Outside the U.S. double this amount. All cassettes and CDs are sent first class and are unconditionally guaranteed. Please allow 10 days for delivery. Fill out address information on other side and send order form, with check, money order, or credit card payment to:

TIME LINE PRODUCTIONS, INC., 222 Minnetonka Avenue South, WAYZATA, MN 55391 (612) 474-1000

CHECK ONE: ☐ MasterCard ☐ VISA ☐ Check ☐ Money Order

Amount to be charged: ____________ Exp. Date: ____________ Account #: ____________

Cardholder's Name: ____________ Signature: ____________

Time Line releases are available at gift shops and music retailers across the country. If you can't find the album you're looking for, ask your local retailer, or use the order form below.

TITLE	Cassettes	QTY	CDs	QTY	TOTAL
The Heritage Collection Volume I	$11.00		$16.00		
Walking With You	$11.00		$16.00		
Beyond a Dream	$11.00		$16.00		
Sharing the Season Volume II	$11.00		$16.00		
Sharing the Season Volume I	$11.00		$16.00		
Threads of Love	$11.00		$16.00		
Storyline	$11.00		$16.00		
Out of Line	$11.00		$16.00		
PUBLISHED SHEET MUSIC OF RECORDINGS					
The Heritage Collection Volume I			$16.00		
"Walking With You" Original Music			$16.00		
Sharing the Season Volume II			$16.00		
Sharing the Season Volume I			$16.00		
"Threads of Love" Title Track			$6.00		
				Sub Total	
				In MN add 6.5% tax	
				Shipping	
				TOTAL	

Shipping in the U.S. is $1.50 for the first item, plus 50 cents for each additional item. Outside the U.S. double this amount. All cassettes and CDs are sent first class and are unconditionally guaranteed. Please allow 10 days for delivery. Fill out address information on other side and send order form, with check, money order, or credit card payment to:

TIME LINE PRODUCTIONS, INC., 222 Minnetonka Avenue South, WAYZATA, MN 55391 (612) 474-1000

CHECK ONE: ☐ MasterCard ☐ VISA ☐ Check ☐ Money Order

Amount to be charged: ____________ Exp. Date: ____________ Account #: ____________

Cardholder's Name: ____________ Signature: ____________

YES! Please put me on your mailing list to receive information regarding future concert dates, new recording releases, and published sheet music.

Name________________________________

Address ________________________________

City ____________________ State ________ Zip ________

Where did you purchase this sheet music? ____________________

What songs would you like to have Lorie publish in the future? ________________

Comments ________________________________

YES! Please put me on your mailing list to receive information regarding future concert dates, new recording releases, and published sheet music.

Name________________________________

Address ________________________________

City ____________________ State ________ Zip ________

Where did you purchase this sheet music? ____________________

What songs would you like to have Lorie publish in the future? ________________

Comments ________________________________